The
⟩HAPPIEST⟨
GRATITUDE
JOURNAL

HAPPY PRESS & CO

This book belongs to: _____

THE HAPPIEST GRATITUDE JOURNAL
365+ DAYS

FROM ARISTOTLE, EINSTEIN AND BUDDHA TO LINCOLN, GANDHI AND OPRAH,
EVERYONE AGREES - EXPRESSING THANKS IS ONE OF THE SIMPLEST
AND MOST EFFECTIVE WAYS TO BE HAPPY.

THIS JOURNAL WAS DESIGNED TO DO JUST THAT - HELP YOU
LEARN TO PUT THIS POWERFUL TECHNIQUE INTO PRACTICE,
SO YOU CAN FIND JOY & HAPPINESS IN EVERYDAY LIFE.

START TODAY AND BE AMAZED HOW LOOKING-ON-THE-BRIGHT-SIDE
FOR FEW MINUTES A DAY CAN TRANSFORM YOUR LIFE FOREVER.

I can change the way I think and this will forever change my life for the better

My progress

To easily see your progress throughout the year, please use this progress-tracking page.

SO FAR I'VE COMPLETED _____ weeks

1	2	3	4	5	6	7	8
9	10	11	12	13	14	15	16
17	18	19	20	21	22	23	24
25	26	27	28	29	30	31	32
33	34	35	36	37	38	39	40
41	42	43	44	45	46	47	48
49	50	51	52	53			

I AM HAPPY BECAUSE I'M GRATEFUL. THAT GRATITUDE ALLOWS ME TO BE HAPPY.

- Will Arnett

Today I am grateful for: DAY 1   ___/___/___

1. _____

2. _____

3. _____

Today I am grateful for: DAY 2   ___/___/___

1. _____

2. _____

3. _____

Today I am grateful for: DAY 3   ___/___/___

1. _____

2. _____

3. _____

Today I am grateful for: DAY 4   ___/___/___

1. _____

2. _____

3. _____

Today I am grateful for: DAY 5   ___/___/___

1. _____

2. _____

3. _____

Today I am grateful for: **DAY 6** ___/___/___

1. _____
2. _____
3. _____

Today I am grateful for: **DAY 7** ___/___/___

1. _____
2. _____
3. _____

This WEEK'S HAPPINESS LEVEL 🙁 🙂 😊 _____

CONTRIBUTING FACTOR(S) _____

TO IMPROVE, I SHOULD _____

Congrats on completing another week! Don't forget to mark week #1 on My Progress page

WHAT ARE YOU GRATEFUL TO HAVE TODAY THAT YOU DIDN'T HAVE *a year ago* ?

_____

_____

notes

NOTHING NEW CAN COME INTO YOUR LIFE UNLESS YOU ARE GRATEFUL FOR WHAT YOU ALREADY HAVE.

- Michael Bernhard

Today I am grateful for: **DAY 8**   ___/___/___

1. _____
2. _____
3. _____

Today I am grateful for: **DAY 9**   ___/___/___

1. _____
2. _____
3. _____

Today I am grateful for: **DAY 10**   ___/___/___

1. _____
2. _____
3. _____

Today I am grateful for: **DAY 11**   ___/___/___

1. _____
2. _____
3. _____

Today I am grateful for: **DAY 12**   ___/___/___

1. _____
2. _____
3. _____

Today I am grateful for: DAY 13   ___/___/___

1. _____
2. _____
3. _____

Today I am grateful for: DAY 14   ___/___/___

1. _____
2. _____
3. _____

This WEEK'S HAPPINESS LEVEL   ☺ ☺ ☺ _____

CONTRIBUTING FACTOR(S) _____

TO IMPROVE, I SHOULD _____

_____
Congrats on completing another week! Don't forget to mark week #2 on My Progress page

WHAT ARE YOU LOOKING FORWARD TO *next week* ?

_____
_____

notes

IF YOU WANT TO FIND HAPPINESS, FIND GRATITUDE.

- Steve Maraboli

Today I am grateful for: **DAY 15**   __/__/__

1. _____

2. _____

3. _____

Today I am grateful for: **DAY 16**   __/__/__

1. _____

2. _____

3. _____

Today I am grateful for: **DAY 17**   __/__/__

1. _____

2. _____

3. _____

Today I am grateful for: **DAY 18**   __/__/__

1. _____

2. _____

3. _____

Today I am grateful for: **DAY 19**   __/__/__

1. _____

2. _____

3. _____

Today I am grateful for:

DAY 20 ___/___/___

1. _____
2. _____
3. _____

Today I am grateful for:

DAY 21 ___/___/___

1. _____
2. _____
3. _____

This WEEK'S HAPPINESS LEVEL ☹ ☺ 😊 _____

CONTRIBUTING FACTOR(S) _____

TO IMPROVE, I SHOULD _____

Congrats on completing another week! Don't forget to mark week #3 on My Progress page

DESCRIBE A *happy* MEMORY

_____

_____

notes

A GRATEFUL HEART IS A BEGINNING OF GREATNESS. IT IS A FOUNDATION FOR THE DEVELOPMENT OF SUCH VIRTUES AS COURAGE, CONTENTMENT, HAPPINESS, LOVE, AND WELL-BEING.

- James E. Faust

Today I am grateful for: DAY 22   ___/___/___

1. _____

2. _____

3. _____

Today I am grateful for: DAY 23   ___/___/___

1. _____

2. _____

3. _____

Today I am grateful for: DAY 24   ___/___/___

1. _____

2. _____

3. _____

Today I am grateful for: DAY 25   ___/___/___

1. _____

2. _____

3. _____

Today I am grateful for: DAY 26   ___/___/___

1. _____

2. _____

3. _____

Today I am grateful for: DAY 27   ___/___/___

1. _____

2. _____

3. _____

Today I am grateful for: DAY 28   ___/___/___

1. _____

2. _____

3. _____

This WEEK'S HAPPINESS LEVEL   😐 🙂 😊   _____

CONTRIBUTING FACTOR(S) _____

TO IMPROVE, I SHOULD _____

Congrats on completing another week! Don't forget to mark week #4 on My Progress page

DESCRIBE A *place* YOU'VE VISITED THAT YOU'RE GRATEFUL FOR

_____

_____

notes

What makes me happy

You can easily increase your happiness level by doing things that make you happy on a more regular basis.

What brings a smile to your face? What gives you energy and excitement? What are you passionate about? What gives your life meaning?

List these things below, give them a score between 1 and 10 and decide how often you'll integrate them into your life - daily, weekly, monthly…

Activity	Score	Frequency

THE HAPPIEST PEOPLE SEEM TO BE THOSE WHO HAVE NO
PARTICULAR CAUSE FOR BEING HAPPY EXCEPT THAT THEY ARE SO.

- William Inge

Today I am grateful for: **DAY 29**   ___/___/___

1. _____
2. _____
3. _____

Today I am grateful for: **DAY 30**   ___/___/___

1. _____
2. _____
3. _____

Today I am grateful for: **DAY 31**   ___/___/___

1. _____
2. _____
3. _____

Today I am grateful for: **DAY 32**   ___/___/___

1. _____
2. _____
3. _____

Today I am grateful for: **DAY 33**   ___/___/___

1. _____
2. _____
3. _____

Today I am grateful for: **DAY 34**   ___/___/___

1. _____

2. _____

3. _____

Today I am grateful for: **DAY 35**   ___/___/___

1. _____

2. _____

3. _____

This WEEK'S HAPPINESS LEVEL   ☺ ☺ ☺ _____

CONTRIBUTING FACTOR(S) _____

TO IMPROVE, I SHOULD _____

Congrats on completing another week! Don't forget to mark week #5 on My Progress page

DESCRIBE AN *accomplishment* YOU'RE PROUD OF

_____

_____

notes

WE TEND TO FORGET THAT HAPPINESS DOESN'T COME AS A RESULT OF GETTING SOMETHING WE DON'T HAVE, BUT RATHER OF RECOGNIZING AND APPRECIATING WHAT WE DO HAVE.

- Frederick Keonig

Today I am grateful for: DAY 36   __/__/__

1. _____

2. _____

3. _____

Today I am grateful for: DAY 37   __/__/__

1. _____

2. _____

3. _____

Today I am grateful for: DAY 38   __/__/__

1. _____

2. _____

3. _____

Today I am grateful for: DAY 39   __/__/__

1. _____

2. _____

3. _____

Today I am grateful for: DAY 40   __/__/__

1. _____

2. _____

3. _____

Today I am grateful for: DAY 41   ___/___/___

1. _____

2. _____

3. _____

Today I am grateful for: DAY 42   ___/___/___

1. _____

2. _____

3. _____

This WEEK'S HAPPINESS LEVEL   ☺ ☺ ☺ _____

CONTRIBUTING FACTOR(S) _____

TO IMPROVE, I SHOULD _____

Congrats on completing another week! Don't forget to mark week #6 on My Progress page

WRITE ABOUT A *special person* IN YOUR LIFE THAT YOU'RE GRATEFUL FOR.

_____

_____

notes

THE SINGLE GREATEST THING YOU CAN DO TO CHANGE YOUR LIFE TODAY WOULD BE TO START BEING GRATEFUL FOR WHAT YOU HAVE RIGHT NOW. AND THE MORE GRATEFUL YOU ARE, THE MORE YOU GET.

- Oprah Winfrey

Today I am grateful for: DAY 43   ___/___/___

1. _____
2. _____
3. _____

Today I am grateful for: DAY 44   ___/___/___

1. _____
2. _____
3. _____

Today I am grateful for: DAY 45   ___/___/___

1. _____
2. _____
3. _____

Today I am grateful for: DAY 46   ___/___/___

1. _____
2. _____
3. _____

Today I am grateful for: DAY 47   ___/___/___

1. _____
2. _____
3. _____

Today I am grateful for:

DAY 48 ___/___/___

1. _____
2. _____
3. _____

Today I am grateful for:

DAY 49 ___/___/___

1. _____
2. _____
3. _____

This WEEK'S HAPPINESS LEVEL :-| :-) :-D _____

CONTRIBUTING FACTOR(S) _____

TO IMPROVE, I SHOULD _____

Congrats on completing another week! Don't forget to mark week #7 on My Progress page

DESCRIBE A *simple* PLEASURE THAT YOU'RE GRATEFUL FOR

_____
_____

notes

FOR EVERY MINUTE YOU ARE ANGRY YOU LOSE SIXTY SECONDS OF HAPPINESS.

- Ralph Waldo Emerson

Today I am grateful for: **DAY 50**   ___/___/___

1. _____
2. _____
3. _____

Today I am grateful for: **DAY 51**   ___/___/___

1. _____
2. _____
3. _____

Today I am grateful for: **DAY 52**   ___/___/___

1. _____
2. _____
3. _____

Today I am grateful for: **DAY 53**   ___/___/___

1. _____
2. _____
3. _____

Today I am grateful for: **DAY 54**   ___/___/___

1. _____
2. _____
3. _____

Today I am grateful for: **DAY 55**   ___/___/___

1. _____

2. _____

3. _____

Today I am grateful for: **DAY 56**   ___/___/___

1. _____

2. _____

3. _____

This WEEK'S HAPPINESS LEVEL   ☺ ☺ ☺   _____

CONTRIBUTING FACTOR(S) _____

TO IMPROVE, I SHOULD _____

_____

Congrats on completing another week! Don't forget to mark week #8 on My Progress page

WHAT ARE YOU LOOKING FORWARD TO *in the next 3 months* ?

_____

_____

notes

3, 2, 1, Go!

IN 60 SECONDS, HOW MANY THINGS CAN YOU LIST THAT YOU ARE GRATEFUL FOR?

You will be amazed!

1. _____
2. _____
3. _____
4. _____
5. _____
6. _____
7. _____
8. _____
9. _____
10. _____
11. _____
12. _____
13. _____
14. _____
15. _____

16. _____
17. _____
18. _____
19. _____
20. _____
21. _____
22. _____
23. _____
24. _____
25. _____
26. _____
27. _____
28. _____
29. _____
30. _____

FOLKS ARE USUALLY ABOUT AS HAPPY AS THEY MAKE THEIR MINDS UP TO BE.

- Abraham Lincoln

Today I am grateful for: DAY 57   ___/___/___

1. _____

2. _____

3. _____

Today I am grateful for: DAY 58   ___/___/___

1. _____

2. _____

3. _____

Today I am grateful for: DAY 59   ___/___/___

1. _____

2. _____

3. _____

Today I am grateful for: DAY 60   ___/___/___

1. _____

2. _____

3. _____

Today I am grateful for: DAY 61   ___/___/___

1. _____

2. _____

3. _____

Today I am grateful for: **DAY 62**   __/__/__

1. _____

2. _____

3. _____

Today I am grateful for: **DAY 63**   __/__/__

1. _____

2. _____

3. _____

This WEEK'S HAPPINESS LEVEL   😐 🙂 😄   _____

CONTRIBUTING FACTOR(S) _____

TO IMPROVE, I SHOULD _____

_____

Congrats on completing another week! Don't forget to mark week #9 on My Progress page

WRITE ABOUT A *Tradition* THAT YOU'RE GRATEFUL FOR

_____

_____

notes

HAPPINESS DEPENDS UPON OURSELVES.

- Aristotle

Today I am grateful for: **DAY 64**   ___/___/___

1. _____

2. _____

3. _____

Today I am grateful for: **DAY 65**   ___/___/___

1. _____

2. _____

3. _____

Today I am grateful for: **DAY 66**   ___/___/___

1. _____

2. _____

3. _____

Today I am grateful for: **DAY 67**   ___/___/___

1. _____

2. _____

3. _____

Today I am grateful for: **DAY 68**   ___/___/___

1. _____

2. _____

3. _____

Today I am grateful for: DAY 69   ___/___/___

1. _____

2. _____

3. _____

Today I am grateful for: DAY 70   ___/___/___

1. _____

2. _____

3. _____

This WEEK'S HAPPINESS LEVEL   🙂 🙂 😊 _____

CONTRIBUTING FACTOR(S) _____

TO IMPROVE, I SHOULD _____

Congrats on completing another week! Don't forget to mark week #10 on My Progress page

WRITE ABOUT YOUR PERSONALITY *Traits* THAT YOU'RE GRATEFUL FOR

_____

_____

notes

THE MOST IMPORTANT THING IS TO ENJOY YOUR LIFE. TO BE HAPPY. IT'S ALL THAT MATTERS.

- Audrey Hepburn

Today I am grateful for: **DAY 71**   ___/___/___

1. _____
2. _____
3. _____

Today I am grateful for: **DAY 72**   ___/___/___

1. _____
2. _____
3. _____

Today I am grateful for: **DAY 73**   ___/___/___

1. _____
2. _____
3. _____

Today I am grateful for: **DAY 74**   ___/___/___

1. _____
2. _____
3. _____

Today I am grateful for: **DAY 75**   ___/___/___

1. _____
2. _____
3. _____

Today I am grateful for: **DAY 76**   ___/___/___

1. _____

2. _____

3. _____

Today I am grateful for: **DAY 77**   ___/___/___

1. _____

2. _____

3. _____

This WEEK'S HAPPINESS LEVEL 😐 🙂 😄 _____

CONTRIBUTING FACTOR(S) _____

TO IMPROVE, I SHOULD _____

_____

Congrats on completing another week! Don't forget to mark week #11 on My Progress page

WHAT *mistakes* OR FAILURES ARE YOU GRATEFUL FOR?

_____

_____

notes

I HAVE ONLY TWO KINDS OF DAYS: HAPPY AND HYSTERICALLY HAPPY.

- Allen J. Lefferdink

Today I am grateful for: **DAY 78**   ___/___/___

1. _____

2. _____

3. _____

Today I am grateful for: **DAY 79**   ___/___/___

1. _____

2. _____

3. _____

Today I am grateful for: **DAY 80**   ___/___/___

1. _____

2. _____

3. _____

Today I am grateful for: **DAY 81**   ___/___/___

1. _____

2. _____

3. _____

Today I am grateful for: **DAY 82**   ___/___/___

1. _____

2. _____

3. _____

Today I am grateful for: DAY 83   __/__/__

1. _____

2. _____

3. _____

Today I am grateful for: DAY 84   __/__/__

1. _____

2. _____

3. _____

This WEEK'S HAPPINESS LEVEL   😐 🙂 😄 _____

CONTRIBUTING FACTOR(S) _____

TO IMPROVE, I SHOULD _____

Congrats on completing another week! Don't forget to mark week #12 on My Progress page

WHAT'S SOMETHING ABOUT YOUR *body/health* THAT YOU'RE GRATEFUL FOR?

_____

_____

notes

Great THINGS are Done BY a series OF small THINGS Brought together.

— VINCENT VAN GOGH

I am grateful

Use the prompts below to identify what you are most grateful for in your life. When we write things down, we often feel more clear-headed and insightful.

I AM GRATEFUL FOR MY...

FAMILY *because* ...

_____

_____

FRIENDS *because* ...

_____

_____

BODY *because* ...

_____

_____

CAREER *because* ...

_____

_____

PAST *because* ...

_____

_____

ABILITIES *to* ...

_____

_____

LOVE *to* ...

_____

_____

ACCESS *to* ...

_____

_____

IF THE ONLY PRAYER YOU EVER SAY IN YOUR ENTIRE LIFE IS THANK YOU, IT WILL BE ENOUGH.

- Meister Eckhart

Today I am grateful for: **DAY 85**   ___/___/___

1. _____
2. _____
3. _____

Today I am grateful for: **DAY 86**   ___/___/___

1. _____
2. _____
3. _____

Today I am grateful for: **DAY 87**   ___/___/___

1. _____
2. _____
3. _____

Today I am grateful for: **DAY 88**   ___/___/___

1. _____
2. _____
3. _____

Today I am grateful for: **DAY 89**   ___/___/___

1. _____
2. _____
3. _____

Today I am grateful for: DAY 90   __/__/__

1. _____
2. _____
3. _____

Today I am grateful for: DAY 91   __/__/__

1. _____
2. _____
3. _____

This WEEK'S HAPPINESS LEVEL   😕 🙂 😄   _____

CONTRIBUTING FACTOR(S) _____

TO IMPROVE, I SHOULD _____

_____
Congrats on completing another week! Don't forget to mark week #13 on My Progress page

OPEN THE DOOR OR WINDOW AND LOOK OUTSIDE. *See anything* TO BE GRATEFUL FOR?

_____
_____

notes

AN ATTITUDE OF GRATITUDE BRINGS GREAT THINGS.

- Yogi Bhajan

Today I am grateful for: **DAY 92**   ___/___/___

1. _____

2. _____

3. _____

Today I am grateful for: **DAY 93**   ___/___/___

1. _____

2. _____

3. _____

Today I am grateful for: **DAY 94**   ___/___/___

1. _____

2. _____

3. _____

Today I am grateful for: **DAY 95**   ___/___/___

1. _____

2. _____

3. _____

Today I am grateful for: **DAY 96**   ___/___/___

1. _____

2. _____

3. _____

Today I am grateful for:

DAY 97 ___/___/___

1. _____

2. _____

3. _____

Today I am grateful for:

DAY 98 ___/___/___

1. _____

2. _____

3. _____

This WEEK'S HAPPINESS LEVEL ☺ ☺ ☺ _____

CONTRIBUTING FACTOR(S) _____

TO IMPROVE, I SHOULD _____

Congrats on completing another week! Don't forget to mark week #14 on My Progress page

WHAT skills DO YOU HAVE THAT YOU'RE GRATEFUL FOR?

_____

_____

notes

HAPPINESS DOES NOT LEAD TO GRATITUDE. GRATITUDE LEADS TO HAPPINESS.

- David Steindl-Rast

Today I am grateful for: **DAY 99**   ___/___/___

1. _____
2. _____
3. _____

Today I am grateful for: *yay!* ⟩ **DAY 100** ⟨ ___/___/___

1. _____
2. _____
3. _____

Today I am grateful for: **DAY 101**   ___/___/___

1. _____
2. _____
3. _____

Today I am grateful for: **DAY 102**   ___/___/___

1. _____
2. _____
3. _____

Today I am grateful for: **DAY 103**   ___/___/___

1. _____
2. _____
3. _____

Today I am grateful for: **DAY 104**   __/__/__

1. _____
2. _____
3. _____

Today I am grateful for: **DAY 105**   __/__/__

1. _____
2. _____
3. _____

This WEEK'S HAPPINESS LEVEL   ☹ 😐 😊 _____

CONTRIBUTING FACTOR(S) _____

TO IMPROVE, I SHOULD _____

Congrats on completing another week! Don't forget to mark week #15 on My Progress page

100 DAYS! *wow!* KEEP UP THE GOOD WORK! ANY THOUGHTS, IDEAS?

_____
_____

notes

WHEN I STARTED COUNTING MY BLESSINGS, MY WHOLE LIFE TURNED AROUND.

- Willie Nelson

Today I am grateful for: **DAY 106**   ___/___/___

1. _____
2. _____
3. _____

Today I am grateful for: **DAY 107**   ___/___/___

1. _____
2. _____
3. _____

Today I am grateful for: **DAY 108**   ___/___/___

1. _____
2. _____
3. _____

Today I am grateful for: **DAY 109**   ___/___/___

1. _____
2. _____
3. _____

Today I am grateful for: **DAY 110**   ___/___/___

1. _____
2. _____
3. _____

Today I am grateful for: **DAY 111**   ___/___/___

1. _____

2. _____

3. _____

Today I am grateful for: **DAY 112**   ___/___/___

1. _____

2. _____

3. _____

This WEEK'S HAPPINESS LEVEL   ☺ ☺ ☺   _____

CONTRIBUTING FACTOR(S) _____

TO IMPROVE, I SHOULD _____

_____
Congrats on completing another week! Don't forget to mark week #16 on My Progress page

WHAT IS YOUR FAVORITE *day* OF THE YEAR AND WHY?

_____

_____

notes

100 days check-in

You are doing great! To recap your journey so far:

3 AMAZING THINGS THAT HAPPENED IN THE PAST 100 DAYS...

_____

_____

_____

I WAS CHALLENGED BY...

_____

_____

_____

I AM PROUD OF MYSELF FOR...

_____

_____

_____

TO MAKE IT EVEN BETTER, IN THE NEXT 100 DAYS I'M GOING TO...

_____

_____

_____

HAPPINESS IS WHEN WHAT YOU THINK, WHAT YOU SAY, AND WHAT YOU DO ARE IN HARMONY.

- Mahatma Gandhi

Today I am grateful for: DAY 113   __/__/__

1. _____
2. _____
3. _____

Today I am grateful for: DAY 114   __/__/__

1. _____
2. _____
3. _____

Today I am grateful for: DAY 115   __/__/__

1. _____
2. _____
3. _____

Today I am grateful for: DAY 116   __/__/__

1. _____
2. _____
3. _____

Today I am grateful for: DAY 117   __/__/__

1. _____
2. _____
3. _____

Today I am grateful for: **DAY 118**   __/__/__

1. _____
2. _____
3. _____

Today I am grateful for: **DAY 119**   __/__/__

1. _____
2. _____
3. _____

This WEEK'S HAPPINESS LEVEL ☺ ☺ ☺ _____

CONTRIBUTING FACTOR(S) _____

TO IMPROVE, I SHOULD _____

_____

Congrats on completing another week! Don't forget to mark week #17 on My Progress page

LOOK AROUND THE ROOM. *See anything* TO BE GRATEFUL FOR?

_____

_____

notes

WANT TO BE HAPPY? STOP TRYING TO BE PERFECT.
- Brené Brown

Today I am grateful for: DAY 120   ___/___/___

1. _____

2. _____

3. _____

Today I am grateful for: DAY 121   ___/___/___

1. _____

2. _____

3. _____

Today I am grateful for: DAY 122   ___/___/___

1. _____

2. _____

3. _____

Today I am grateful for: DAY 123   ___/___/___

1. _____

2. _____

3. _____

Today I am grateful for: DAY 124   ___/___/___

1. _____

2. _____

3. _____

Today I am grateful for: **DAY 125** ___/___/___

1. _____
2. _____
3. _____

Today I am grateful for: **DAY 126** ___/___/___

1. _____
2. _____
3. _____

This WEEK'S HAPPINESS LEVEL ☹ ☺ 😊 _____

CONTRIBUTING FACTOR(S) _____

TO IMPROVE, I SHOULD _____

_____

Congrats on completing another week! Don't forget to mark week #18 on My Progress page

WRITE INSTRUCTIONS *To a child* ON HOW TO FIND HAPPINESS

_____

_____

notes

PLENTY OF PEOPLE MISS THEIR SHARE OF HAPPINESS, NOT BECAUSE THEY NEVER FOUND IT, BUT BECAUSE THEY DIDN'T STOP TO ENJOY IT.

- William Feather

Today I am grateful for: DAY 127   ___/___/___

1. _____
2. _____
3. _____

Today I am grateful for: DAY 128   ___/___/___

1. _____
2. _____
3. _____

Today I am grateful for: DAY 129   ___/___/___

1. _____
2. _____
3. _____

Today I am grateful for: DAY 130   ___/___/___

1. _____
2. _____
3. _____

Today I am grateful for: DAY 131   ___/___/___

1. _____
2. _____
3. _____

Today I am grateful for: **DAY 132**   ___/___/___

1. _____

2. _____

3. _____

Today I am grateful for: **DAY 133**   ___/___/___

1. _____

2. _____

3. _____

This WEEK'S HAPPINESS LEVEL   ☺ ☺ ☺   _____

CONTRIBUTING FACTOR(S) _____

TO IMPROVE, I SHOULD _____

_____

Congrats on completing another week! Don't forget to mark week #19 on My Progress page

WHAT DO YOU APPRECIATE *most* ABOUT YOUR LIFE RIGHT NOW?

_____

_____

notes

HAPPINESS CANNOT BE TRAVELED TO, OWNED, EARNED, WORN OR CONSUMED. HAPPINESS IS THE SPIRITUAL EXPERIENCE OF LIVING EVERY MINUTE WITH LOVE, GRACE, AND GRATITUDE.

- Denis Waitley

Today I am grateful for: DAY 134   ___/___/___

1. _____
2. _____
3. _____

Today I am grateful for: DAY 135   ___/___/___

1. _____
2. _____
3. _____

Today I am grateful for: DAY 136   ___/___/___

1. _____
2. _____
3. _____

Today I am grateful for: DAY 137   ___/___/___

1. _____
2. _____
3. _____

Today I am grateful for: DAY 138   ___/___/___

1. _____
2. _____
3. _____

Today I am grateful for: **DAY 139** ___/___/___

1. _____

2. _____

3. _____

Today I am grateful for: **DAY 140** ___/___/___

1. _____

2. _____

3. _____

This WEEK'S HAPPINESS LEVEL 😕 🙂 😄 _____

CONTRIBUTING FACTOR(S) _____

TO IMPROVE, I SHOULD _____

Congrats on completing another week! Don't forget to mark week #20 on My Progress page

WHAT WOULD YOUR *Teenage* SELF LOVE ABOUT YOU NOW?

_____

_____

notes

Make others feel good

When we make others feel good about themselves, we feel a sense of bliss.
Showing gratitude more frequently is also a way of building others up.

There are many ways we can show gratitude to the people in our lives.
List them below:

_____

_____

_____

_____

_____

_____

_____

_____

_____

_____

_____

_____

_____

DO NOT SET ASIDE YOUR HAPPINESS. DO NOT WAIT TO BE HAPPY IN THE FUTURE. THE BEST TIME TO BE HAPPY IS ALWAYS NOW.

- Roy T. Bennett

Today I am grateful for: DAY 141   ___/___/___

1. _____
2. _____
3. _____

Today I am grateful for: DAY 142   ___/___/___

1. _____
2. _____
3. _____

Today I am grateful for: DAY 143   ___/___/___

1. _____
2. _____
3. _____

Today I am grateful for: DAY 144   ___/___/___

1. _____
2. _____
3. _____

Today I am grateful for: DAY 145   ___/___/___

1. _____
2. _____
3. _____

Today I am grateful for: **DAY 146**   ___/___/___

1. _____

2. _____

3. _____

Today I am grateful for: **DAY 147**   ___/___/___

1. _____

2. _____

3. _____

This **WEEK'S HAPPINESS LEVEL**   (☹) (☺) (😊) _____

CONTRIBUTING FACTOR(S) _____

TO IMPROVE, I SHOULD _____

Congrats on completing another week! Don't forget to mark week #21 on My Progress page

WHAT "HAPPINESS" MEANS *to you* ?

_____

_____

notes

HAPPINESS IS THE SECRET TO ALL BEAUTY. THERE IS NO BEAUTY WITHOUT HAPPINESS.

- Christian Dior

Today I am grateful for:

DAY 148 ___/___/___

1. _____
2. _____
3. _____

Today I am grateful for:

DAY 149 ___/___/___

1. _____
2. _____
3. _____

Today I am grateful for:

DAY 150 ___/___/___

1. _____
2. _____
3. _____

Today I am grateful for:

DAY 151 ___/___/___

1. _____
2. _____
3. _____

Today I am grateful for:

DAY 152 ___/___/___

1. _____
2. _____
3. _____

Today I am grateful for: DAY 153 ___/___/___

1. _____
2. _____
3. _____

Today I am grateful for: DAY 154 ___/___/___

1. _____
2. _____
3. _____

This WEEK'S HAPPINESS LEVEL 😐 🙂 😊 _____

CONTRIBUTING FACTOR(S) _____

TO IMPROVE, I SHOULD _____

Congrats on completing another week! Don't forget to mark week #22 on My Progress page

WHAT IS *one privilege* YOU HAVE THAT YOU OFTEN TAKE FOR GRANTED?

_____
_____

notes

OPTIMISM IS THE ONE QUALITY MORE ASSOCIATED WITH SUCCESS AND HAPPINESS THAN ANY OTHER.

- Brian Tracy

Today I am grateful for: DAY 155   __/__/__

1. _____
2. _____
3. _____

Today I am grateful for: DAY 156   __/__/__

1. _____
2. _____
3. _____

Today I am grateful for: DAY 157   __/__/__

1. _____
2. _____
3. _____

Today I am grateful for: DAY 158   __/__/__

1. _____
2. _____
3. _____

Today I am grateful for: DAY 159   __/__/__

1. _____
2. _____
3. _____

Today I am grateful for: **DAY 160**   __/__/__

1. _____

2. _____

3. _____

Today I am grateful for: **DAY 161**   __/__/__

1. _____

2. _____

3. _____

This WEEK'S HAPPINESS LEVEL   :·(:·) :·D _____

CONTRIBUTING FACTOR(S) _____

TO IMPROVE, I SHOULD _____

Congrats on completing another week! Don't forget to mark week #23 on My Progress page

I FEEL *happiest* WHEN...

_____

_____

notes

GIVE THANKS FOR A LITTLE, AND YOU WILL FIND A LOT.

- Hausa Proverb

Today I am grateful for: DAY 162   ___/___/___

1. _____
2. _____
3. _____

Today I am grateful for: DAY 163   ___/___/___

1. _____
2. _____
3. _____

Today I am grateful for: DAY 164   ___/___/___

1. _____
2. _____
3. _____

Today I am grateful for: DAY 165   ___/___/___

1. _____
2. _____
3. _____

Today I am grateful for: DAY 166   ___/___/___

1. _____
2. _____
3. _____

Today I am grateful for: DAY 167   ___/___/___

1. _____

2. _____

3. _____

Today I am grateful for: DAY 168   ___/___/___

1. _____

2. _____

3. _____

This WEEK'S HAPPINESS LEVEL   ☹ ☺ 😄 _____

CONTRIBUTING FACTOR(S) _____

TO IMPROVE, I SHOULD _____

Congrats on completing another week! Don't forget to mark week #24 on My Progress page

WHAT IS SOMETHING YOU NEED TO FORGIVE YOURSELF FOR? WRITE IT DOWN AND BE *done with it*

_____

_____

notes

"DO NOT WISH TO BE ANYTHING BUT WHAT YOU ARE, AND TRY TO BE THAT PERFECTLY."

– ST. FRANCIS DE SALES

Reverse gratitude

Every event in life happens to teach us something.
Sometimes the lessons are bittersweet, but they're part of the journey.

In order to gain strength, we need to experience pain. In order to grow, we need
to go through discomfort. In order to have peace of mind, we need to let go.

FAILURES, MISTAKES, DIFFICULTIES, OR CHALLENGING EVENTS ...

WHAT DO THEY TEACH ME? WHAT DID I LEARN?

THE STRUGGLE ENDS WHEN GRATITUDE BEGINS.

- Neale Donald Walsh

Today I am grateful for: DAY 169   ___/___/___

1. _____

2. _____

3. _____

Today I am grateful for: DAY 170   ___/___/___

1. _____

2. _____

3. _____

Today I am grateful for: DAY 171   ___/___/___

1. _____

2. _____

3. _____

Today I am grateful for: DAY 172   ___/___/___

1. _____

2. _____

3. _____

Today I am grateful for: DAY 173   ___/___/___

1. _____

2. _____

3. _____

Today I am grateful for: DAY 174   ___/___/___

1. _____

2. _____

3. _____

Today I am grateful for: DAY 175   ___/___/___

1. _____

2. _____

3. _____

This WEEK'S HAPPINESS LEVEL ☺ ☺ ☺ _____

CONTRIBUTING FACTOR(S) _____

TO IMPROVE, I SHOULD _____

_____

Congrats on completing another week! Don't forget to mark week #25 on My Progress page

WHO WOULD YOU LIKE TO SPEND MORE TIME WITH? WHAT ARE *some ways* YOU COULD DO THAT?

_____

_____

notes

BE THANKFUL FOR WHAT YOU HAVE. YOUR LIFE IS SOMEONE ELSE'S FAIRY TALE.

- Wale Ayeni

Today I am grateful for: **DAY 176**   ___/___/___

1. _____
2. _____
3. _____

Today I am grateful for: **DAY 177**   ___/___/___

1. _____
2. _____
3. _____

Today I am grateful for: **DAY 178**   ___/___/___

1. _____
2. _____
3. _____

Today I am grateful for: **DAY 179**   ___/___/___

1. _____
2. _____
3. _____

Today I am grateful for: **DAY 180**   ___/___/___

1. _____
2. _____
3. _____

Today I am grateful for: DAY 181   __/__/__

1. _____

2. _____

3. _____

Today I am grateful for: DAY 182   __/__/__

1. _____

2. _____

3. _____

This WEEK'S HAPPINESS LEVEL 😕 🙂 😄 _____

CONTRIBUTING FACTOR(S) _____

TO IMPROVE, I SHOULD _____

Congrats on completing another week! Don't forget to mark week #26 on My Progress page

WHAT ARE SOME SKILLS YOU HAVE ALWAYS *wanted* TO LEARN?

_____

_____

notes

Today I am grateful for: DAY 183   ___/___/___

1. _____

2. _____

3. _____

Today I am grateful for: DAY 184   ___/___/___

1. _____

2. _____

3. _____

Today I am grateful for: DAY 185   ___/___/___

1. _____

2. _____

3. _____

Today I am grateful for: DAY 186   ___/___/___

1. _____

2. _____

3. _____

Today I am grateful for: DAY 187   ___/___/___

1. _____

2. _____

3. _____

Today I am grateful for: **DAY 188**   ___/___/___

1. _____
2. _____
3. _____

Today I am grateful for: **DAY 189**   ___/___/___

1. _____
2. _____
3. _____

This WEEK'S HAPPINESS LEVEL   😐 🙂 😄   _____

CONTRIBUTING FACTOR(S) _____

TO IMPROVE, I SHOULD _____

Congrats on completing another week! Don't forget to mark week #27 on My Progress page

who MADE YOUR LIFE BETTER THIS WEEK?

_____
_____

notes

THERE ARE ONLY TWO WAYS TO LIVE YOUR LIVE. ONE IS AS THOUGH NOTHING IS A MIRACLE. THE OTHER AS IS THOUGH EVERYTHING IS A MIRACLE.

- Albert Einstein

Today I am grateful for: **DAY 190**   ___/___/___

1. _____
2. _____
3. _____

Today I am grateful for: **DAY 191**   ___/___/___

1. _____
2. _____
3. _____

Today I am grateful for: **DAY 192**   ___/___/___

1. _____
2. _____
3. _____

Today I am grateful for: **DAY 193**   ___/___/___

1. _____
2. _____
3. _____

Today I am grateful for: **DAY 194**   ___/___/___

1. _____
2. _____
3. _____

Today I am grateful for: **DAY 195**   ___/___/___

1. _____
2. _____
3. _____

Today I am grateful for: **DAY 196**   ___/___/___

1. _____
2. _____
3. _____

This WEEK'S HAPPINESS LEVEL   ☹ ☺ 😊 _____

CONTRIBUTING FACTOR(S) _____

TO IMPROVE, I SHOULD _____

Congrats on completing another week! Don't forget to mark week #28 on My Progress page

WRITE ABOUT A *family* MEMBER THAT YOU'RE GRATEFUL FOR

_____
_____

notes

Rise above the storm and you will find the sunshine.

Don't take it for granted

Sometimes we take things for granted
because we imagine they'll always be there.

But what if those things or people did not exist the way they do in our lives?
Practicing this kind of awareness and gratitude can help us put things into greater perspective.

What things or relationships do you take for granted and would really miss if they were gone?

_____

_____

_____

_____

_____

_____

_____

_____

_____

_____

_____

_____

_____

HAPPINESS IS NOT IN THINGS; IT IS IN YOU.

- Robert Holden

Today I am grateful for: DAY 197   ___/___/___

1. _____

2. _____

3. _____

Today I am grateful for: DAY 198   ___/___/___

1. _____

2. _____

3. _____

Today I am grateful for: DAY 199   ___/___/___

1. _____

2. _____

3. _____

Today I am grateful for: wow! ⋛DAY 200⋚ ___/___/___

1. _____

2. _____

3. _____

Today I am grateful for: DAY 201   ___/___/___

1. _____

2. _____

3. _____

Today I am grateful for: **DAY 202** ___/___/___

1. _____
2. _____
3. _____

Today I am grateful for: **DAY 203** ___/___/___

1. _____
2. _____
3. _____

This WEEK'S HAPPINESS LEVEL ☹ ☺ 😊 _____

CONTRIBUTING FACTOR(S) _____

TO IMPROVE, I SHOULD _____

Congrats on completing another week! Don't forget to mark week #29 on My Progress page

200 DAYS! *awesome job!* YOU'RE DOING IT! ANY THOUGHTS, IDEAS?

_____
_____

notes

VERY LITTLE IS NEEDED TO MAKE A HAPPY LIFE. IT IS ALL WITHIN YOURSELF IN YOUR WAY OF THINKING.

- Marcus Aurelius

Today I am grateful for: DAY 204   ___/___/___

1. _____
2. _____
3. _____

Today I am grateful for: DAY 205   ___/___/___

1. _____
2. _____
3. _____

Today I am grateful for: DAY 206   ___/___/___

1. _____
2. _____
3. _____

Today I am grateful for: DAY 207   ___/___/___

1. _____
2. _____
3. _____

Today I am grateful for: DAY 208   ___/___/___

1. _____
2. _____
3. _____

Today I am grateful for: **DAY 209** ___/___/___

1. _____

2. _____

3. _____

Today I am grateful for: **DAY 210** ___/___/___

1. _____

2. _____

3. _____

This WEEK'S HAPPINESS LEVEL ☺ ☺ ☺ _____

CONTRIBUTING FACTOR(S) _____

TO IMPROVE, I SHOULD _____

_____

Congrats on completing another week! Don't forget to mark week #30 on My Progress page

BEST THING THAT HAPPENED *this week* WAS...

_____

_____

notes

HAPPINESS IS AN INSIDE JOB. DON'T ASSIGN ANYONE ELSE THAT MUCH POWER OVER YOUR LIFE.

- Mandy Hale

Today I am grateful for: DAY 211 ___/___/___

1. _____
2. _____
3. _____

Today I am grateful for: DAY 212 ___/___/___

1. _____
2. _____
3. _____

Today I am grateful for: DAY 213 ___/___/___

1. _____
2. _____
3. _____

Today I am grateful for: DAY 214 ___/___/___

1. _____
2. _____
3. _____

Today I am grateful for: DAY 215 ___/___/___

1. _____
2. _____
3. _____

Today I am grateful for: **DAY 216**   ___/___/___

1. _____
2. _____
3. _____

Today I am grateful for: **DAY 217**   ___/___/___

1. _____
2. _____
3. _____

This WEEK'S HAPPINESS LEVEL   🙁 🙂 😄   _____

CONTRIBUTING FACTOR(S) _____

TO IMPROVE, I SHOULD _____

Congrats on completing another week! Don't forget to mark week #31 on My Progress page

OPEN YOUR PHONE FIND *a photo* THAT YOU LIKE. WHY ARE YOU GRATEFUL FOR THIS PHOTO?

_____
_____

notes

THE CONSTITUTION ONLY GUARANTEES YOU THE RIGHT TO PURSUE HAPPINESS. YOU HAVE TO CATCH IT YOURSELF.

- Benjamin Franklin

Today I am grateful for:

DAY 218 ___/___/___

1. _____
2. _____
3. _____

Today I am grateful for:

DAY 219 ___/___/___

1. _____
2. _____
3. _____

Today I am grateful for:

DAY 220 ___/___/___

1. _____
2. _____
3. _____

Today I am grateful for:

DAY 221 ___/___/___

1. _____
2. _____
3. _____

Today I am grateful for:

DAY 222 ___/___/___

1. _____
2. _____
3. _____

Today I am grateful for: **DAY 223**   ___/___/___

1. _____

2. _____

3. _____

Today I am grateful for: **DAY 224**   ___/___/___

1. _____

2. _____

3. _____

This WEEK'S HAPPINESS LEVEL   ☺ ☺ ☺   _____

CONTRIBUTING FACTOR(S) _____

TO IMPROVE, I SHOULD _____

_____

Congrats on completing another week! Don't forget to mark week #32 on My Progress page

HOW CAN YOU MAKE NEXT WEEK *awesome*?

_____

_____

notes

Sometimes we just need to be our own hero.

200 days check-in

You are doing great! To recap your journey so far:

3 AMAZING THINGS THAT HAPPENED IN THE PAST 100 DAYS...

_____

_____

_____

I WAS CHALLENGED BY...

_____

_____

_____

I AM PROUD OF MYSELF FOR...

_____

_____

_____

TO MAKE IT EVEN BETTER, IN THE NEXT 100 DAYS I'M GOING TO...

_____

_____

_____

SUCCESS IS NOT THE KEY TO HAPPINESS, HAPPINESS IS THE KEY TO SUCCESS.

- Herman Cain

Today I am grateful for: **DAY 225**   ___/___/___

1. _____

2. _____

3. _____

Today I am grateful for: **DAY 226**   ___/___/___

1. _____

2. _____

3. _____

Today I am grateful for: **DAY 227**   ___/___/___

1. _____

2. _____

3. _____

Today I am grateful for: **DAY 228**   ___/___/___

1. _____

2. _____

3. _____

Today I am grateful for: **DAY 229**   ___/___/___

1. _____

2. _____

3. _____

Today I am grateful for:　　　　　　　　　　　　　DAY 230　　___/___/___

1. _____

2. _____

3. _____

Today I am grateful for:　　　　　　　　　　　　　DAY 231　　___/___/___

1. _____

2. _____

3. _____

This WEEK'S HAPPINESS LEVEL　　😕 🙂 😄　　_____

CONTRIBUTING FACTOR(S) _____

TO IMPROVE, I SHOULD _____

_____

Congrats on completing another week! Don't forget to mark week #33 on My Progress page

WHAT'S SOMETHING THAT YOU *bought* RECENTLY THAT YOU'RE GRATEFUL FOR?

_____

_____

notes

AT THE AGE OF 18, I MADE UP MY MIND TO NEVER HAVE ANOTHER BAD DAY IN MY LIFE. I DOVE INTO A ENDLESS SEA OF GRATITUDE FROM WHICH I'VE NEVER EMERGED.

- Patch Adams

Today I am grateful for: DAY 232   ___/___/___

1. _____
2. _____
3. _____

Today I am grateful for: DAY 233   ___/___/___

1. _____
2. _____
3. _____

Today I am grateful for: DAY 234   ___/___/___

1. _____
2. _____
3. _____

Today I am grateful for: DAY 235   ___/___/___

1. _____
2. _____
3. _____

Today I am grateful for: DAY 236   ___/___/___

1. _____
2. _____
3. _____

Today I am grateful for: DAY 237 __/__/__

1. _____
2. _____
3. _____

Today I am grateful for: DAY 238 __/__/__

1. _____
2. _____
3. _____

This WEEK'S HAPPINESS LEVEL 😕 🙂 😄 _____

CONTRIBUTING FACTOR(S) _____

TO IMPROVE, I SHOULD _____

_____

Congrats on completing another week! Don't forget to mark week #34 on My Progress page

what CAN YOU BE GRATEFUL FOR THAT HAS CHANGED OR IMPROVED IN THE PAST 6 MONTHS?

_____
_____

notes

HAPPINESS DOESN'T DEPEND ON WHAT WE HAVE, BUT IT DOES DEPEND ON HOW WE FEEL TOWARD WHAT WE HAVE. WE CAN BE HAPPY WITH LITTLE AND MISERABLE WITH MUCH.

- William D. Hoard

Today I am grateful for: DAY 239   ___/___/___

1. _____

2. _____

3. _____

Today I am grateful for: DAY 240   ___/___/___

1. _____

2. _____

3. _____

Today I am grateful for: DAY 241   ___/___/___

1. _____

2. _____

3. _____

Today I am grateful for: DAY 242   ___/___/___

1. _____

2. _____

3. _____

Today I am grateful for: DAY 243   ___/___/___

1. _____

2. _____

3. _____

Today I am grateful for: **DAY 244** ___ / ___ / ___

1. _____
2. _____
3. _____

Today I am grateful for: **DAY 245** ___ / ___ / ___

1. _____
2. _____
3. _____

This WEEK'S HAPPINESS LEVEL :-(:-) :-D _____

CONTRIBUTING FACTOR(S) _____

TO IMPROVE, I SHOULD _____

Congrats on completing another week! Don't forget to mark week #35 on My Progress page

WHAT *strengths* OR ABILITIES DO YOU HAVE THAT YOU ARE MOST GRATEFUL FOR?

_____
_____

notes

OPTIMISM IS A HAPPINESS MAGNET. IF YOU STAY POSITIVE, GOOD THINGS AND GOOD PEOPLE WILL BE DRAWN TO YOU.

- Mary Lou Retton

Today I am grateful for: DAY 246   ___/___/___

1. _____

2. _____

3. _____

Today I am grateful for: DAY 247   ___/___/___

1. _____

2. _____

3. _____

Today I am grateful for: DAY 248   ___/___/___

1. _____

2. _____

3. _____

Today I am grateful for: DAY 249   ___/___/___

1. _____

2. _____

3. _____

Today I am grateful for: DAY 250   ___/___/___

1. _____

2. _____

3. _____

Today I am grateful for: DAY 251   ___/___/___

1. _____

2. _____

3. _____

Today I am grateful for: DAY 252   ___/___/___

1. _____

2. _____

3. _____

This WEEK'S HAPPINESS LEVEL   ☺ ☺ ☺   _____

CONTRIBUTING FACTOR(S) _____

TO IMPROVE, I SHOULD _____

Congrats on completing another week! Don't forget to mark week #36 on My Progress page

WHAT IS ONE UNIQUE *thing* YOU APPRECIATE ABOUT YOURSELF?

_____

_____

notes

I AM STRONG
STRONGER THAN I REALIZE

The gratitude game

Gratitude is a very powerful tool.
It not only turns what we already have into enough,
but it also has the power to bring more good into our lives.

Think of gratitude as a magnet.
As we hold the magnet in our hands and give thanks for it,
it begins to attract more of what we want in our lives.
The more gratitude we give, the more powerful the magnet gets.

LIST 4 THINGS THAT YOU ARE GRATEFUL FOR FROM *last* 30 DAYS:

1. _____
2. _____
3. _____
4. _____

LIST 4 THINGS THAT YOU'D BE GRATEFUL FOR IF THEY CAME TRUE IN *next* 30 DAYS:

1. _____
2. _____
3. _____
4. _____

IT ISN'T WHAT YOU HAVE, OR WHO YOU ARE, OR WHERE YOU ARE, OR WHAT YOU ARE DOING THAT MAKES YOU HAPPY OR UNHAPPY. IT IS WHAT YOU THINK ABOUT.

- Dale Carnegie

Today I am grateful for: DAY 253   __/__/__

1. _____

2. _____

3. _____

Today I am grateful for: DAY 254   __/__/__

1. _____

2. _____

3. _____

Today I am grateful for: DAY 255   __/__/__

1. _____

2. _____

3. _____

Today I am grateful for: DAY 256   __/__/__

1. _____

2. _____

3. _____

Today I am grateful for: DAY 257   __/__/__

1. _____

2. _____

3. _____

Today I am grateful for: **DAY 258**   ___/___/___

1. _____
2. _____
3. _____

Today I am grateful for: **DAY 259**   ___/___/___

1. _____
2. _____
3. _____

This WEEK'S HAPPINESS LEVEL   ☹ ☺ ☺   _____

CONTRIBUTING FACTOR(S) _____

TO IMPROVE, I SHOULD _____

_____

Congrats on completing another week! Don't forget to mark week #37 on My Progress page

who HAS HAD THE GREATEST IMPACT ON SHAPING THE PERSON YOU HAVE BECOME?

_____
_____

notes

GRATITUDE IS A POWERFUL PROCESS FOR SHIFTING YOUR ENERGY AND BRINGING MORE OF WHAT YOU WANT INTO YOUR LIFE. BE GRATEFUL FOR WHAT YOU ALREADY HAVE AND YOU WILL ATTRACT MORE GOOD THINGS.

- Rhonda Byrne

Today I am grateful for: DAY 260   __/__/__

1. _____
2. _____
3. _____

Today I am grateful for: DAY 261   __/__/__

1. _____
2. _____
3. _____

Today I am grateful for: DAY 262   __/__/__

1. _____
2. _____
3. _____

Today I am grateful for: DAY 263   __/__/__

1. _____
2. _____
3. _____

Today I am grateful for: DAY 264   __/__/__

1. _____
2. _____
3. _____

Today I am grateful for: DAY 265   ___/___/___

1. _____

2. _____

3. _____

Today I am grateful for: DAY 266   ___/___/___

1. _____

2. _____

3. _____

This WEEK'S HAPPINESS LEVEL   :(:) :D   _____

CONTRIBUTING FACTOR(S) _____

TO IMPROVE, I SHOULD _____

_____

Congrats on completing another week! Don't forget to mark week #38 on My Progress page

what MADE YOUR LIFE EASIER THIS WEEK?

_____

_____

notes

WHEN GRATITUDE BECOMES AN ESSENTIAL FOUNDATION IN OUR LIVES, MIRACLES START TO APPEAR EVERYWHERE.

- Emmanuel Dalgher

Today I am grateful for: **DAY 267**   __/__/__

1. _____
2. _____
3. _____

Today I am grateful for: **DAY 268**   __/__/__

1. _____
2. _____
3. _____

Today I am grateful for: **DAY 269**   __/__/__

1. _____
2. _____
3. _____

Today I am grateful for: **DAY 270**   __/__/__

1. _____
2. _____
3. _____

Today I am grateful for: **DAY 271**   __/__/__

1. _____
2. _____
3. _____

Today I am grateful for: DAY 272   ___/___/___

1. _____

2. _____

3. _____

Today I am grateful for: DAY 273   ___/___/___

1. _____

2. _____

3. _____

This WEEK'S HAPPINESS LEVEL 😕 🙂 😄 _____

CONTRIBUTING FACTOR(S) _____

TO IMPROVE, I SHOULD _____

Congrats on completing another week! Don't forget to mark week #39 on My Progress page

WHAT opportunities ARE YOU THANKFUL FOR?

_____

_____

notes

GRATITUDE UNLOCKS ALL THAT'S BLOCKING US FROM REALLY FEELING TRUTHFUL, REALLY FEELING AUTHENTIC AND HAPPY.

- Gabrielle Bernstein

Today I am grateful for: DAY 274   ___/___/___

1. _____

2. _____

3. _____

Today I am grateful for: DAY 275   ___/___/___

1. _____

2. _____

3. _____

Today I am grateful for: DAY 276   ___/___/___

1. _____

2. _____

3. _____

Today I am grateful for: DAY 277   ___/___/___

1. _____

2. _____

3. _____

Today I am grateful for: DAY 278   ___/___/___

1. _____

2. _____

3. _____

Today I am grateful for:

DAY 279 ___/___/___

1. _____
2. _____
3. _____

Today I am grateful for:

DAY 280 ___/___/___

1. _____
2. _____
3. _____

This WEEK'S HAPPINESS LEVEL 😕 🙂 😄 _____

CONTRIBUTING FACTOR(S) _____

TO IMPROVE, I SHOULD _____

Congrats on completing another week! Don't forget to mark week #40 on My Progress page

WHAT ADVERSITY HAVE YOU FACED IN YOUR LIFE THAT ULTIMATELY BECAME *a blessing*?

_____

_____

notes

COURAGE,
DEAR HEART

The gratitude letter

DEAR

_____

I THANK YOU BECAUSE

_____

_____

_____

I LOVE THESE QUALITIES ABOUT YOU

_____

_____

_____

I AM GRATEFUL FOR YOUR HELP & SUPPORT WITH

_____

_____

_____

I HOPE THAT

_____

_____

WHEN YOU ARISE IN THE MORNING, THINK OF WHAT A PRECIOUS PRIVILEGE IT IS TO BE ALIVE — TO BREATHE, TO THINK, TO ENJOY, TO LOVE.

- Marcus Aurelius

Today I am grateful for: DAY 281   ___/___/___

1. _____
2. _____
3. _____

Today I am grateful for: DAY 282   ___/___/___

1. _____
2. _____
3. _____

Today I am grateful for: DAY 283   ___/___/___

1. _____
2. _____
3. _____

Today I am grateful for: DAY 284   ___/___/___

1. _____
2. _____
3. _____

Today I am grateful for: DAY 285   ___/___/___

1. _____
2. _____
3. _____

Today I am grateful for: DAY 286   __/__/__

1. _____

2. _____

3. _____

Today I am grateful for: DAY 287   __/__/__

1. _____

2. _____

3. _____

This WEEK'S HAPPINESS LEVEL :·) :·) :·) _____

CONTRIBUTING FACTOR(S) _____

TO IMPROVE, I SHOULD _____

Congrats on completing another week! Don't forget to mark week #41 on My Progress page

WHAT *kind acts* HAVE MADE YOU FEEL MORE GRATEFUL?

_____

_____

notes

IT IS ONLY WITH GRATITUDE THAT LIFE BECOMES RICH.

- Deitrich Bonheiffer

Today I am grateful for: DAY 288   __/__/__

1. _____
2. _____
3. _____

Today I am grateful for: DAY 289   __/__/__

1. _____
2. _____
3. _____

Today I am grateful for: DAY 290   __/__/__

1. _____
2. _____
3. _____

Today I am grateful for: DAY 291   __/__/__

1. _____
2. _____
3. _____

Today I am grateful for: DAY 292   __/__/__

1. _____
2. _____
3. _____

Today I am grateful for: DAY 293   ___/___/___

1. _____

2. _____

3. _____

Today I am grateful for: DAY 294   ___/___/___

1. _____

2. _____

3. _____

This WEEK'S HAPPINESS LEVEL   :·) :·) :·) _____

CONTRIBUTING FACTOR(S) _____

TO IMPROVE, I SHOULD _____

Congrats on completing another week! Don't forget to mark week #42 on My Progress page

WHICH *relationships* ARE YOU MOST GRATEFUL FOR IN YOUR LIFE?

_____

_____

notes

THROUGH THE EYES OF GRATITUDE, EVERYTHING IS A MIRACLE.

- Mary Davis

Today I am grateful for: DAY 295   ___/___/___

1. _____

2. _____

3. _____

Today I am grateful for: DAY 296   ___/___/___

1. _____

2. _____

3. _____

Today I am grateful for: DAY 297   ___/___/___

1. _____

2. _____

3. _____

Today I am grateful for: DAY 298   ___/___/___

1. _____

2. _____

3. _____

Today I am grateful for: DAY 299   ___/___/___

1. _____

2. _____

3. _____

Today I am grateful for:

awesome! ⋛DAY 300⋚ ___/___/___

1. _____
2. _____
3. _____

Today I am grateful for:

DAY 301 ___/___/___

1. _____
2. _____
3. _____

This WEEK'S HAPPINESS LEVEL ☹ ☺ 😊 _____

CONTRIBUTING FACTOR(S) _____

TO IMPROVE, I SHOULD _____

Congrats on completing another week! Don't forget to mark week #43 on My Progress page

300 DAYS! *how about that?!!* **YOU'RE A PRO NOW! ANY THOUGHTS, IDEAS?**

_____
_____

notes

THE ROOT OF JOY IS GRATEFULNESS.

- David Steindl-Rast

Today I am grateful for: DAY 302   ___/___/___

1. _____

2. _____

3. _____

Today I am grateful for: DAY 303   ___/___/___

1. _____

2. _____

3. _____

Today I am grateful for: DAY 304   ___/___/___

1. _____

2. _____

3. _____

Today I am grateful for: DAY 305   ___/___/___

1. _____

2. _____

3. _____

Today I am grateful for: DAY 306   ___/___/___

1. _____

2. _____

3. _____

Today I am grateful for:

DAY 307 ___/___/___

1. _____
2. _____
3. _____

Today I am grateful for:

DAY 308 ___/___/___

1. _____
2. _____
3. _____

This WEEK'S HAPPINESS LEVEL ☹ ☺ 😊 _____

CONTRIBUTING FACTOR(S) _____

TO IMPROVE, I SHOULD _____

_____

Congrats on completing another week! Don't forget to mark week #44 on My Progress page

WHAT IS one thing THAT MAKES YOUR LIFE EASIER EVERY DAY?

_____

_____

notes

300 days check-in

You are doing great! To recap your journey so far:

3 AMAZING THINGS THAT HAPPENED IN THE PAST 100 DAYS...

_____

_____

_____

I WAS CHALLENGED BY...

_____

_____

_____

I AM PROUD OF MYSELF FOR...

_____

_____

_____

TO MAKE IT EVEN BETTER, IN THE NEXT 100 DAYS I'M GOING TO...

_____

_____

_____

GRATITUDE IS AN OPENER OF LOCKED-UP BLESSINGS.

- Marianne Williamson

Today I am grateful for: **DAY 309** ___/___/___

1. _____
2. _____
3. _____

Today I am grateful for: **DAY 310** ___/___/___

1. _____
2. _____
3. _____

Today I am grateful for: **DAY 311** ___/___/___

1. _____
2. _____
3. _____

Today I am grateful for: **DAY 312** ___/___/___

1. _____
2. _____
3. _____

Today I am grateful for: **DAY 313** ___/___/___

1. _____
2. _____
3. _____

Today I am grateful for:

DAY 314 ___/___/___

1. _____
2. _____
3. _____

Today I am grateful for:

DAY 315 ___/___/___

1. _____
2. _____
3. _____

This WEEK'S HAPPINESS LEVEL 😕 🙂 😄 _____

CONTRIBUTING FACTOR(S) _____

TO IMPROVE, I SHOULD _____

_____

Congrats on completing another week! Don't forget to mark week #45 on My Progress page

DESCRIBE YOUR HAPPIEST *childhood* MEMORY

_____

_____

notes

**CHOOSING TO BE POSITIVE AND HAVING A GRATEFUL ATTITUDE
IS GOING TO DETERMINE HOW YOU'RE GOING TO LIVE YOUR LIFE.**

- Joel Osteen

Today I am grateful for: DAY 316   __/__/__

1. _____
2. _____
3. _____

Today I am grateful for: DAY 317   __/__/__

1. _____
2. _____
3. _____

Today I am grateful for: DAY 318   __/__/__

1. _____
2. _____
3. _____

Today I am grateful for: DAY 319   __/__/__

1. _____
2. _____
3. _____

Today I am grateful for: DAY 320   __/__/__

1. _____
2. _____
3. _____

Today I am grateful for: DAY 321 ___/___/___

1. _____

2. _____

3. _____

Today I am grateful for: DAY 322 ___/___/___

1. _____

2. _____

3. _____

This WEEK'S HAPPINESS LEVEL ☹ ☺ 😄 _____

CONTRIBUTING FACTOR(S) _____

TO IMPROVE, I SHOULD _____

Congrats on completing another week! Don't forget to mark week #46 on My Progress page

WHAT DO YOU *love most* ABOUT THE CITY YOU LIVE IN?

_____

_____

notes

IT'S NOT POSSIBLE TO EXPERIENCE CONSTANT EUPHORIA, BUT IF YOU'RE GRATEFUL, YOU CAN FIND HAPPINESS IN EVERYTHING.

- Pharrell Williams

Today I am grateful for: DAY 323   ___/___/___

1. _____

2. _____

3. _____

Today I am grateful for: DAY 324   ___/___/___

1. _____

2. _____

3. _____

Today I am grateful for: DAY 325   ___/___/___

1. _____

2. _____

3. _____

Today I am grateful for: DAY 326   ___/___/___

1. _____

2. _____

3. _____

Today I am grateful for: DAY 327   ___/___/___

1. _____

2. _____

3. _____

Today I am grateful for: DAY 328   __/__/__

1. _____
2. _____
3. _____

Today I am grateful for: DAY 329   __/__/__

1. _____
2. _____
3. _____

This WEEK'S HAPPINESS LEVEL   :·) :·) :·) _____

CONTRIBUTING FACTOR(S) _____

TO IMPROVE, I SHOULD _____

Congrats on completing another week! Don't forget to mark week #47 on My Progress page

BEST THING THAT HAPPENED *this week* WAS...

_____
_____

notes

I DON'T HAVE TO CHASE EXTRAORDINARY MOMENTS TO FIND HAPPINESS – IT'S RIGHT IN FRONT OF ME IF I'M PAYING ATTENTION AND PRACTICING GRATITUDE.

- Brene Brown

Today I am grateful for: DAY 330   ___/___/___

1. _____

2. _____

3. _____

Today I am grateful for: DAY 331   ___/___/___

1. _____

2. _____

3. _____

Today I am grateful for: DAY 332   ___/___/___

1. _____

2. _____

3. _____

Today I am grateful for: DAY 333   ___/___/___

1. _____

2. _____

3. _____

Today I am grateful for: DAY 334   ___/___/___

1. _____

2. _____

3. _____

Today I am grateful for: DAY 335   __/__/__

1. _____

2. _____

3. _____

Today I am grateful for: DAY 336   __/__/__

1. _____

2. _____

3. _____

This WEEK'S HAPPINESS LEVEL   ☺ ☺ ☺   _____

CONTRIBUTING FACTOR(S) _____

TO IMPROVE, I SHOULD _____

_____

Congrats on completing another week! Don't forget to mark week #48 on My Progress page

WHAT ARE SOME OF THE SIMPLE, EVERYDAY *Things* THAT MAKE YOU FEEL HAPPY?

_____

_____

notes

OF THIS BE SURE: YOU DO NOT FIND THE HAPPY LIFE...YOU MAKE IT.

- Thomas S. Monson

Today I am grateful for: DAY 337   __/__/__

1. _____
2. _____
3. _____

Today I am grateful for: DAY 338   __/__/__

1. _____
2. _____
3. _____

Today I am grateful for: DAY 339   __/__/__

1. _____
2. _____
3. _____

Today I am grateful for: DAY 340   __/__/__

1. _____
2. _____
3. _____

Today I am grateful for: DAY 341   __/__/__

1. _____
2. _____
3. _____

Today I am grateful for: **DAY 342**   ___/___/___

1. _____

2. _____

3. _____

Today I am grateful for: **DAY 343**   ___/___/___

1. _____

2. _____

3. _____

This WEEK'S HAPPINESS LEVEL   😕 🙂 😄   _____

CONTRIBUTING FACTOR(S) _____

TO IMPROVE, I SHOULD _____

WHAT IS *something* YOU'VE TAKEN FOR GRANTED THAT YOU COULD BE MORE GRATEFUL FOR?

_____

_____

notes

IF YOU WANT TO BE HAPPY, BE.

- Leo Tolstoy

Today I am grateful for: DAY 344   ___/___/___

1. _____

2. _____

3. _____

Today I am grateful for: DAY 345   ___/___/___

1. _____

2. _____

3. _____

Today I am grateful for: DAY 346   ___/___/___

1. _____

2. _____

3. _____

Today I am grateful for: DAY 347   ___/___/___

1. _____

2. _____

3. _____

Today I am grateful for: DAY 348   ___/___/___

1. _____

2. _____

3. _____

Today I am grateful for: DAY 349   __/__/__

1. _____

2. _____

3. _____

Today I am grateful for: DAY 350   __/__/__

1. _____

2. _____

3. _____

This WEEK'S HAPPINESS LEVEL   ☺ ☺ ☺   _____

CONTRIBUTING FACTOR(S) _____

TO IMPROVE, I SHOULD _____

Congrats on completing another week! Don't forget to mark week #50 on My Progress page

WHAT ARE *some ways* YOU COULD SHARE MORE GRATITUDE WITH OTHERS?

_____

_____

notes

HAPPINESS IS A HABIT. CULTIVATE IT.
- Elbert Hubbard

Today I am grateful for: DAY 351   ___/___/___

1. _____
2. _____
3. _____

Today I am grateful for: DAY 352   ___/___/___

1. _____
2. _____
3. _____

Today I am grateful for: DAY 353   ___/___/___

1. _____
2. _____
3. _____

Today I am grateful for: DAY 354   ___/___/___

1. _____
2. _____
3. _____

Today I am grateful for: DAY 355   ___/___/___

1. _____
2. _____
3. _____

Today I am grateful for: DAY 356   __/__/__

1. _____

2. _____

3. _____

Today I am grateful for: DAY 357   __/__/__

1. _____

2. _____

3. _____

This WEEK'S HAPPINESS LEVEL ☹ ☺ 😊 _____

CONTRIBUTING FACTOR(S) _____

TO IMPROVE, I SHOULD _____

Congrats on completing another week! Don't forget to mark week #51 on My Progress page

WHAT HAVE YOU LEARNED ABOUT *yourself* OVER THE LAST 30 DAYS?

_____

_____

notes

UNTIL YOU ARE HAPPY WITH WHO YOU ARE, YOU WILL NEVER BE HAPPY WITH WHAT YOU HAVE.

- Zig Ziglar

Today I am grateful for: DAY 358   __/__/__

1. _____
2. _____
3. _____

Today I am grateful for: DAY 359   __/__/__

1. _____
2. _____
3. _____

Today I am grateful for: DAY 360   __/__/__

1. _____
2. _____
3. _____

Today I am grateful for: DAY 361   __/__/__

1. _____
2. _____
3. _____

Today I am grateful for: DAY 362   __/__/__

1. _____
2. _____
3. _____

Today I am grateful for: **DAY 363**   ___/___/___

1. _____

2. _____

3. _____

Today I am grateful for: **DAY 364**   ___/___/___

1. _____

2. _____

3. _____

This WEEK'S HAPPINESS LEVEL   😐 🙂 😄   _____

CONTRIBUTING FACTOR(S) _____

TO IMPROVE, I SHOULD _____

Congrats on completing another week! Don't forget to mark week #52 on My Progress page

WHAT HAVE YOU LEARNED ABOUT *yourself* OVER THE LAST YEAR?

_____

_____

notes

LIVING IN A STATE OF GRATITUDE IS THE GATEWAY TO GRACE.
- Arianna Huffington

Today I am grateful for:

one whole year! >DAY 365< ___/___/___

1. _____
2. _____
3. _____

Today I am grateful for:

DAY 366   ___/___/___

1. _____
2. _____
3. _____

Today I am grateful for:

DAY 367   ___/___/___

1. _____
2. _____
3. _____

Today I am grateful for:

DAY 368   ___/___/___

1. _____
2. _____
3. _____

Today I am grateful for:

DAY 369   ___/___/___

1. _____
2. _____
3. _____

Today I am grateful for: **DAY 370**   ___/___/___

1. _____
2. _____
3. _____

Today I am grateful for: **DAY 371**   ___/___/___

1. _____
2. _____
3. _____

This WEEK'S HAPPINESS LEVEL   ☺ ☺ ☺   _____

CONTRIBUTING FACTOR(S) _____

TO IMPROVE, I SHOULD _____

_____

Congrats on completing another week! Don't forget to mark week #53 on My Progress page

YOU ARE NOW A REAL *gratitude wizard* !

_____

_____

notes

Printed in Great Britain
by Amazon

80387370R00079